Transformations in Nature

A Larva
Becomes a Fly

Amy Hayes

Cavendish
Square

New York

Published in 2016 by Cavendish Square Publishing, LLC
243 5th Avenue, Suite 136, New York, NY 10016

Cataloging-in-Publication Data

Hayes, Amy.
A larvae becomes a fly / by Amy Hayes.
p. cm. — (Transformations in nature)
Includes index.
ISBN 978-1-5026-0832-1 (hardcover) ISBN 978-1-5026-0830-7 (paperback) ISBN 978-1-5026-0833-8 (e-book)
1. Flies — Juvenile literature. 2. Flies — Life cycles — Juvenile literature. I. Hayes, Amy. II. Title.
QL533.2 H39 2016
595.77'4—d23

Editorial Director: David McNamara
Copy Editor: Rebecca Rohan
Art Director: Jeffrey Talbot
Designer: Stephanie Flecha
Senior Production Manager: Jennifer Ryder-Talbot
Production Editor: Renni Johnson
Photo Research: J8 Media

Printed in the United States of America

Contents

A Larva Turns into a Fly **4**

New Words **22**

Index **23**

About the Author **24**

A **larva** turns into a fly.

5

More than one larva
are called **larvae**.

7

First, a mother lays her eggs.

9

The eggs hatch into larvae.

11

Larvae eat and eat
for about a week.

Larvae that are full make a red **covering**.

15

This red shell is
called a **pupa**.

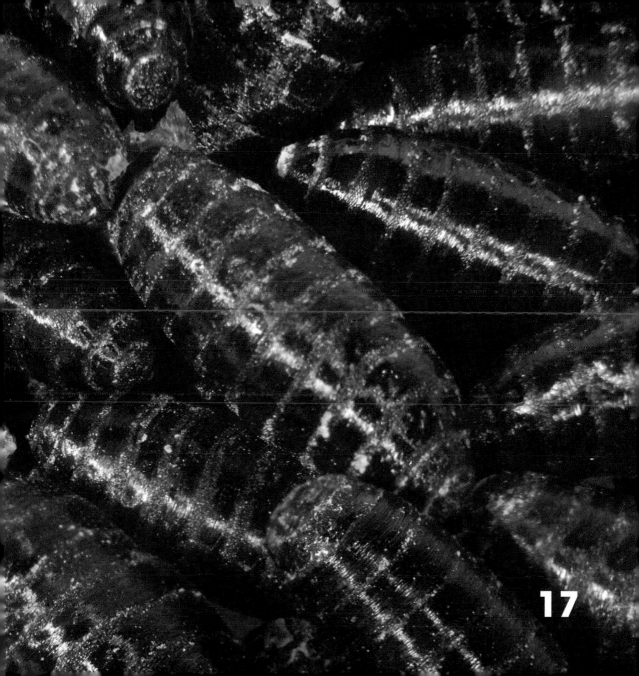
17

After a few weeks,
the pupa breaks open.

18

19

A fly comes out!

20

21

New Words

covering (KOV-er-ing) Something that goes over the larva to protect it.

larva (LAR-va) A very young insect that looks like a worm.

larvae (LAR-vay) More than one larva.

pupa (PEW-pa) Insects in a transformation stage, usually inside a cocoon.

Index

covering, 14

eggs, 8, 10

fly, 4, 20

larva, 4, 6

larvae, 6, 10, 12, 14

pupa, 16, 18

23

About the Author

Amy Hayes lives in the beautiful city of Buffalo, New York. She has written several books for children, including *Hornets*, *Medusa and Pegasus*, *From Wax to Crayons*, and *We Need Worms!*

About BOOKWORMS

Bookworms help independent readers gain reading confidence through high-frequency words, simple sentences, and strong picture/text support. Each book explores a concept that helps children relate what they read to the world they live in.